Pebble™ Plus

Dinosaurs and Prehistoric Animals

Apatosaurus

by Carol K. Lindeen

Consulting Editor: Gail Saunders-Smith, PhD
Consultant: Jack Horner, Curator of Paleontology
Museum of the Rockies
Bozeman, Montana

Capstone
press

Mankato, Minnesota

Pebble Plus is published by Capstone Press,
151 Good Counsel Drive, P.O. Box 669, Mankato, Minnesota 56002.
www.capstonepress.com

1 2 3 4 5 6 10 09 08 07 06 05

Library of Congress Cataloging-in-Publication Data
Lindeen, Carol K., 1976–
    Apatosaurus / by Carol K. Lindeen.
    p. cm.—(Pebble plus. Dinosaurs and prehistoric animals)
    Includes bibliographical references and index.
    Summary: "Simple text and illustrations present the life of apatosaurus, how it looked, and
its behavior."—Provided by publisher.
    ISBN 0-7368-4256-X (hardcover)
    1. Apatosaurus—Juvenile literature. I. Title. II. Series.
QE862.S3L493 2006
567.913—dc22   2004026741

Editorial Credits
Sarah L. Schuette, editor; Linda Clavel, set designer; Bobbi J. Dey, book designer; Wanda Winch, photo researcher

Illustration and Photo Credits
Jon Hughes, illustrator
David Liebman, 21

Note to Parents and Teachers

The Dinosaurs and Prehistoric Animals set supports national science standards related
to the evolution of life. This book describes and illustrates apatosaurus. The images
support early readers in understanding the text. The repetition of words and phrases
helps early readers learn new words. This book also introduces early readers to
subject-specific vocabulary words, which are defined in the Glossary section. Early
readers may need assistance to read some words and to use the Table of Contents,
Glossary, Read More, Internet Sites, and Index sections of the book.

Table of Contents

A Long Dinosaur

Apatosaurus was

a very long dinosaur.

It had a long neck

and a long tail.

Apatosaurus lived
in prehistoric times.
It lived about 150 million
years ago in western
North America.

How Apatosaurus Looked

Apatosaurus was as long
as two school buses.
It was about 70 feet
(21 meters) long.

Apatosaurus had
strong, thick legs.
It walked slowly.

Apatosaurus had
a long, thin tail.
It held its tail
off the ground.

What Apatosaurus Did

Apatosaurus needed to eat
a lot of food.
It spent most of the day
eating from treetops.

Apatosaurus tore food off

trees with its teeth.

It had teeth

shaped like pegs.

Apatosaurus swallowed

its food whole.

It did not chew.

The End of Apatosaurus

The last apatosaurus died

about 145 million years ago.

No one knows

why they all died.

You can see apatosaurus

fossils in museums.

Glossary

dinosaur—a large reptile that lived on land in prehistoric times

fossil—the remains or traces of an animal or a plant, preserved as rock

museum—a place where objects of art, history, or science are shown

prehistoric—very, very old; prehistoric means belonging to a time before history was written down.

Read More

Cohen, Daniel. *Apatosaurus.* Discovering Dinosaurs. Mankato, Minn.: Bridgestone Books, 2001.

Dahl, Michael. *Long-Neck: The Adventure of Apatosaurus.* Dinosaur World. Minneapolis: Picture Window Books, 2004.

Matthews, Rupert. *Apatosaurus.* Gone Forever! Chicago: Heinemann Library, 2004.

Internet Sites

FactHound offers a safe, fun way to find Internet sites related to this book. All of the sites on FactHound have been researched by our staff.

Here's how:

1. Visit *www.facthound.com*

2. Type in this special code **073684256X** for age-appropriate sites. Or enter a search word related to this book for a more general search.

3. Click on the **Fetch It** button.

FactHound will fetch the best sites for you!

Index

Word Count: 131
Grade: 1
Early-Intervention Level: 15